Book

A Strange

Reading Practice

–tion

action	formation
motion	function
fraction	elation
reaction	information
introduction	invitation
addition	irritation
caption	jubilation
caution	punctuation
creation	hesitation
direction	

Contents

Chapter 1 Volcano Village   *page 1*

Chapter 2 Furry Nation   *page 4*

Chapter 3 Mutation   *page 8*

Chapter 4 Good Vibrations   *page 12*

Vocabulary

motion – movement

prediction – a forecast, tell the future

destination – a place to which someone is travelling

anticipation – expecting something

desolation – a feeling of great sadness

elation – great joy

pathetic – pitiful

determination – deciding on a purpose

desperation – being desperate

mutation – extreme transformation of nature

eruption – a violent outburst

jubilation – feeling of joy

devastation – wreckage caused by a destructive event

Chapter 1: Volcano Village

With a rocking motion, Titan stopped at a volcanic island. The symbol on the skyshard looked like a huge eye under some tufts of fur.

"A wild beast?" muttered Finn to himself. Not much of an invitation. He decided not to mention his prediction to Korus.

in vi ta tion   pre dic tion

He gazed upwards. Strange caves clung to the sides of the volcano. Was this really their destination? A thousand sad eyes peered out at them from the shadows.

"What a strange location..." Finn thought.

des ti na tion   lo ca tion

With a shuddering action, Titan pointed a rocky finger in the direction of a path. It snaked up the side of the volcano. "Titan's giving us an instruction!" cried Finn in astonishment. His eyes glowed with excitement. He leapt off Titan in anticipation of adventure.

in struc tion   an ti ci pa tion

Chapter 2: Furry Nation

A mob of furry beings burst from the shadows and swarmed around them. "These furballs have more hair than Salty!" joked Finn. Then he made a surprising observation. "They only have one eye!" Korus looked at them with distrust. "A little more caution is my suggestion!" he warned.

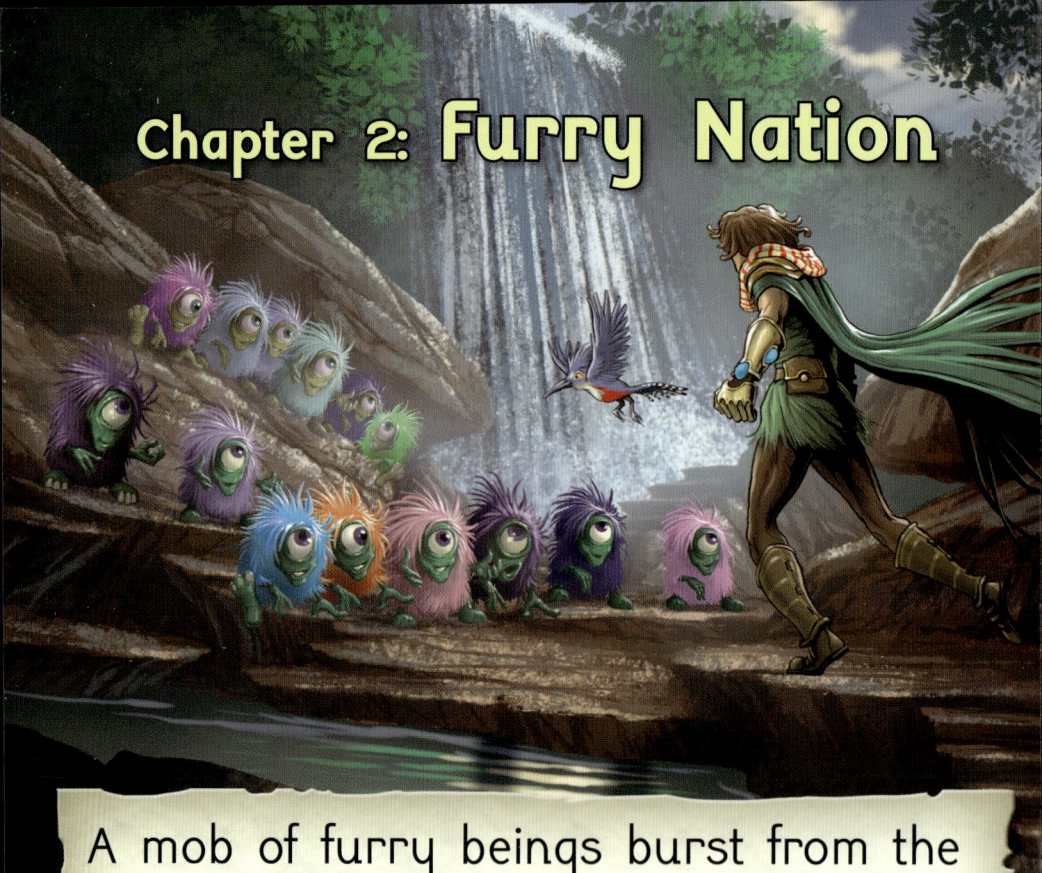

ob ser va tion su gges tion

Finn sensed a terrible desolation coming from the furballs. Korus was still very wary of them. He plucked a fish from the water. The one-eyed furballs watched his every move.

"I might mention here that they seem very hungry," he said.

des o la tion

The furballs gazed at the fish glumly. Finn had a sudden realisation. "They are on the verge of starvation!" he cried. Korus looked up at the island's green vegetation. He made a suggestion. "We could teach them to weave fishing nets from vines!"

re a li sa tion   ve ge ta tion

The nets were a great solution! The furballs caught many fish. "Let's have a celebration meal!" chirped Korus happily. At the campfire, the oldest furball presented Finn with a necklace. The skyshard was hanging from it. "Yes!" yelled Finn, punching the air with elation.

ce leb ra tion   e la tion

Chapter 3: Mutation

Finn had a terrible sensation that he was being watched. Suddenly, an evil cackle echoed from the darkness. A tide of fearful faces turned towards the dark hole in the rockface above them. "What's happening?" shouted Finn. He was confused by their reaction.

re ac tion

Suddenly, a one-eyed mutant beast burst out of the dark space. In one sweeping action, he grabbed the oldest furball in his fist. "These pathetic creatures only eat when I allow it!" he bellowed. "That necklace is my creation and the skyshard is MINE!"

ac tion   path e tic

A sickening crunch followed as the beast crushed the wounded furball in his hand. The monster loomed over the furballs. Finn whispered a horrified observation. "The beast is hypnotising them! Look at their eyes! We have no option, Korus. We must escape!"

| ob ser va tion | hy no ti sing |

The creatures rose as a unified pack. They were now in opposition to Finn. Their brows furrowed in concentration as they grasped at Finn. They marched toward him with determination.

"We must get out!" yelled Finn.

con cen tra tion   de ter mi na tion

Chapter 4: Good Vibrations

"Aim the gauntlets at the rocks on the cliffside!" screeched Korus in desperation. Finn had no option. He must face this mutant that had enslaved these poor creatures. He raised his fists defiantly.

des per a tion

The gauntlets sent out wave after wave of powerful vibrations. The mutant swivelled his terrible eye upwards. He saw the eruption of the crumbling cliff-face above him. It was too late for him to escape. Jagged rocks rained down on him.

vi bra tion   e rup tion

The monster closed his eye as the massive rocks encased him.

"The hypnosis has been broken!" screeched Korus in jubilation. Finn was looking at the devastation around him. Dazed furballs staggered in all directions.

| hyp no sis | ju bi la tion | dev as ta tion |

Finn cradled the wounded furball with affection. "We must take him with us!" he declared without hesitation. A sea of furballs surged gently forward to collect their friend.

"He belongs here," said Korus in gentle explanation. Behind them a twisted hand emerged from the pile of broken rocks.

hes i ta tion   ex pla na tion

The mutant beast burst from the rocks and made a last lunge towards Finn. "Hammer the ground!" screeched Korus. With one powerful motion, Finn opened up a jagged crack in the ground. The beast plummeted into the bubbling lava. A hundred excited furballs cheered and hooted with admiration!

plumm et ed   ad mi ra tion